Table of Content

Chapter 1: Introduction

- Definition of Taekwondo and its significance in the world of sports

Taekwondo is a Korean martial art characterized by its emphasis on high kicks, jumping, and spinning techniques. It is also known for its fluid and powerful movements, making it an exciting and impressive sport to watch. Taekwondo was developed in the 1940s and 1950s by various martial artists in South Korea, and it has since become a popular and widely practiced sport around the world.

One of the defining features of Taekwondo is its focus on both physical and mental discipline. Practitioners of Taekwondo are not only trained in various kicking and punching techniques, but they also learn important values such as respect, humility, and self-control. This focus on character development sets Taekwondo apart from other martial arts and has made it an attractive option for individuals seeking to develop both their physical and mental abilities.

In addition to its cultural significance, Taekwondo also holds an important place in the world of sports. The sport has been featured in the Olympic Games since 2000, and it has continued to grow in popularity and recognition on the global stage. Taekwondo is a highly competitive sport, with athletes competing in various weight classes and demonstrating their skill, speed, and agility in dynamic and fast-paced matches.

The significance of Taekwondo in the world of sports is further highlighted by the stories of athletes who have overcome significant obstacles to achieve success in the sport. From physical injuries to financial challenges, many Taekwondo athletes have faced adversity on their journey to reaching the highest levels of competition. Their stories of determination, perseverance, and triumph are an inspiration to individuals both inside and outside of the Taekwondo community.

Ultimately, Taekwondo's significance in the world of sports lies not only in its athletic prowess and competitive nature, but also in the values and principles that it embodies. As a sport that emphasizes discipline, respect, and perseverance, Taekwondo serves as a powerful platform for individuals to develop both as athletes and as individuals. It is through the dedication and passion of its practitioners that Taekwondo continues to make a lasting impact in the world of sports.

~ Brief history of Taekwondo and its evolution in the Olympic Games

Taekwondo is a Korean martial art that dates back over 2,000 years. The exact origin of the martial art is shrouded in mystery, as much of its history has been passed down through oral tradition. However, it is widely believed that the practice of Taekwondo can be traced back to the ancient Korean kingdoms of Goguryeo, Baekje, and Silla.

The art of Taekwondo is heavily influenced by the indigenous martial arts of Korea, as well as Chinese martial arts. Throughout its history, Taekwondo has evolved to incorporate a wide range of striking techniques, including kicks, punches, and elbow and knee strikes. In addition to its focus on striking techniques, Taekwondo also emphasizes the use of powerful, dynamic movements to generate speed and power.

Throughout the centuries, Taekwondo has remained an integral part of Korean culture, and it has continued to evolve and flourish. In 1955, the Korean government officially recognized Taekwondo as a national martial art, and the first Taekwondo academy, the Korea Taekwondo Association, was established. Over the years, Taekwondo has spread around the world, becoming one of the most popular martial arts in the Olympics.

Taekwondo made its Olympic debut as a demonstration sport at the 1988 Summer Olympics in Seoul, South Korea. Following its successful demonstration, Taekwondo was officially added to the Olympic program as a full medal sport at the 2000 Summer Olympics in Sydney, Australia. Since then, Taekwondo has been a regular feature at the Summer Olympics, with athletes competing in various weight categories for both men and women.

The inclusion of Taekwondo in the Olympics has played a crucial role in popularizing the martial art on a global scale. The exposure provided by the Olympic Games has helped to elevate the status of Taekwondo, and it has provided a platform for athletes to showcase their skills and compete at the highest level.

In recent years, the Olympic format of Taekwondo has continued to evolve, with changes to the scoring system and rules designed to make the sport more dynamic and engaging for spectators. With a focus on high-flying kicks and lightning-fast movements, Taekwondo has become a thrilling and adrenaline-pumping event at the Olympic Games.

Overall, the history of Taekwondo and its evolution in the Olympic Games is a testament to the enduring legacy of this ancient martial art. From its humble origins in Korea to its international prominence, Taekwondo has demonstrated its ability to transcend cultural boundaries and inspire athletes to pursue their Olympic dreams. As Taekwondo continues to evolve and grow, it will undoubtedly remain a source of inspiration and empowerment for athletes around the world.

Chapter 2: The Power of Faith

In the world of sports, achieving success and realizing one's Olympic dreams requires much more than just physical strength and skill. It also demands an unwavering belief in oneself and a firm faith that anything is possible with hard work and dedication. This chapter explores the powerful role that faith has played in the lives of athletes pursuing their Olympic dreams through the practice of Taekwondo.

Many athletes who have achieved greatness in their respective sports attribute a large part of their success to their faith. For some, it is a deeply rooted religious belief that guides and sustains them through their trials and triumphs. For others, it is a more general sense of belief in themselves and their abilities. .

One such athlete is Maria, a Taekwondo practitioner whose faith in God has been a driving force in her journey to the Olympics. Maria grew up in a tough neighborhood, facing adversity and hardship on a daily basis. However, thanks to the guidance of her parents and the support of her faith community, Maria was able to stay focused on her goals and pursue her passion for Taekwondo. She credits her unwavering belief in God's plan for her life as the foundation that has kept her grounded and motivated, even in the face of challenges.

Similarly, Jason, another Taekwondo athlete, has also relied on his faith to overcome obstacles and keep him on the path to achieving his Olympic dreams. Jason's journey has been fraught with setbacks and disappointments, but through it all, his faith in himself and his abilities has never wavered. He often recalls how his belief in the power of hard work and perseverance, fueled by his faith, has enabled him to push through pain and doubt and emerge stronger and more resolute than ever.

The stories of Maria and Jason are just two examples of how the power of faith can shape an athlete's journey to greatness. It is a force that transcends the physical realm and taps into the spiritual and emotional strength that is essential for overcoming obstacles and achieving one's goals. Whether it is a belief in a divine plan or an unyielding trust in oneself, faith has the power to inspire and sustain athletes as they pursue their Olympic dreams through the practice of Taekwondo.

As the reader delves deeper into the narratives of these athletes, it becomes clear that their faith is not just a passive belief that sits in the background, but an active force that propels them forward even when the odds are stacked against them. Through their experiences, the reader gains insight into the transformative power of faith and how it can be a guiding light in the pursuit of greatness.

It is a testament to the enduring power of belief and the resiliency it provides in the face of challenges. The stories of Maria and Jason serve as inspiration for readers, reminding them that with faith, anything is possible.

~ Story of an athlete who faced numerous setbacks but found strength and perseverance through faith

Jonathan was a promising young athlete with dreams of representing his country in the Olympics. As a teenager, he showed great talent and dedication to Taekwondo, and it seemed like nothing could stop him from achieving his goal. However, life had other plans for him.

At the age of 17, Jonathan suffered a devastating knee injury during a competition. The doctors told him that he would never be able to compete again, let alone pursue his Olympic dreams. It was a crushing blow for the young athlete, and he fell into a deep depression.

For months, Jonathan struggled to come to terms with the reality of his situation. He felt lost and unsure of what to do with his life now that his lifelong passion had been taken away from him. It was a dark and difficult time for him, but through the support of his family and friends, he found the strength to keep fighting.

Despite the doctor's prognosis, Jonathan refused to give up on his dream. He underwent multiple surgeries and spent countless hours in rehabilitation, determined to defy the odds and make a comeback. It was a slow and painful process, but with each small victory, Jonathan felt a glimmer of hope and a renewed sense of purpose.

Through his struggles, Jonathan turned to his faith for guidance and support. He found solace in prayer and meditation, and it helped him to keep pushing forward, even when the road ahead seemed daunting and impossible. His faith became a source of strength and perseverance, allowing him to overcome the physical and emotional challenges in his path.

After years of hard work and determination, Jonathan finally made his return to the competitive arena. It was a triumphant moment for him and everyone who had supported him along the way. Despite the setback, he was able to qualify for the national Taekwondo team and eventually represent his country in the Olympics.

It was a long and arduous journey, but through his unwavering faith and relentless determination, Jonathan was able to achieve his childhood dream. His story serves as a powerful reminder that no setback is insurmountable if you have the courage and faith to keep moving forward. He is an inspiration to all aspiring athletes who face obstacles on their path to success.

- Examination of how belief in oneself can lead to achieving Olympic dreams

Belief in oneself is a powerful force that can propel athletes to achieve their Olympic dreams. In the sport of Taekwondo, this belief is especially crucial as athletes face physical, mental, and emotional challenges in their pursuit of excellence.

Many of the athletes featured in the book have faced seemingly insurmountable obstacles on their journey to the Olympics. Whether it be injuries, financial hardship, or doubt from others, these athletes have had to rely on their unwavering belief in themselves to overcome these challenges. Through their unwavering self-belief, they harnessed the strength and resilience necessary to push past the barriers standing in the way of their Olympic dreams.

One such story is that of a young Taekwondo athlete who suffered a career-threatening injury that left him questioning whether he would ever be able to compete at the elite level again. Despite the doubts and naysayers, he maintained an unyielding belief in his ability to overcome his injury and return stronger than ever. Through sheer determination and self-belief, he not only recovered from his injury but went on to achieve his Olympic dreams, standing on the podium and hearing his national anthem play as he received his gold medal.

These stories provide a gripping insight into the transformative power of self-belief, demonstrating how it can fuel an athlete's passion, determination, and perseverance, ultimately leading them to succeed in the face of adversity. It serves as a powerful reminder that belief in oneself is not only a mindset but also a driving force that can make the seemingly impossible possible.

Through the personal accounts of Taekwondo athletes, the book brings to light the profound influence of believing in oneself, underlining its capacity to drive athletes towards their Olympic aspirations. It is an invaluable resource for anyone seeking inspiration and a deeper understanding of the pivotal role that self-belief plays in achieving greatness in the world of sports.

Chapter 3: Resilience and Determination

Kiera's story shows how resilience and determination are crucial elements in the pursuit of Olympic glory.

The chapter details Kiera's early struggles in the sport, including injuries and financial constraints that made it difficult for her to continue competing. Despite these challenges, Kiera never lost sight of her goal and continued to train relentlessly, often sacrificing personal comforts and social outings to focus on her taekwondo practice.

Readers will be inspired by Kiera's unwavering determination and willingness to face adversity head-on. Her story serves as a powerful reminder that success in taekwondo, as in life, often requires the strength to overcome obstacles and push through difficult times.

In addition to Kiera, this section of the book features several other athletes whose stories exemplify the resilience and determination required to succeed in taekwondo. Each athlete's journey is unique, but all share a common thread of overcoming adversity and refusing to be deterred by life's challenges.

The profiles in this section serve as a reminder that triumph in taekwondo is not solely about physical prowess, but also about mental fortitude and the ability to bounce back from setbacks. These real-life examples of resilience and determination will resonate with readers of all ages and backgrounds, providing inspiration and encouragement to persevere in their own pursuits.

Through the tales of these athletes, readers will gain a deeper appreciation for the qualities of resilience and determination, and be inspired to cultivate these traits in themselves. Whether facing obstacles in their athletic endeavors or in other aspects of life, readers will learn valuable lessons from the unwavering spirit of the athletes profiled in this section.

Readers will be captivated by the stories of these athletes and motivated to apply their lessons to their own lives, making this section an invaluable source of inspiration and empowerment.

~ Inspirational tale of an athlete who refused to give up despite facing countless challenges in their journey to the Olympics

In the world of sports, competition is fierce and the road to success is often lined with obstacles. Athletes are constantly pushing themselves to the limit, overcoming challenges, and striving to reach the top of their field. One such athlete who has demonstrated remarkable perseverance and resilience is Alex, a taekwondo practitioner who refused to give up on his dream of competing in the Olympics despite facing countless challenges along the way.

Growing up in a rough neighborhood, Alex was drawn to the discipline and grace of taekwondo at a young age. Despite the lack of resources and support, he began training in a local gym, honing his skills and pushing himself to excel in the sport. However, as he progressed in his training, Alex encountered numerous setbacks that could have easily derailed his aspirations.

In his teenage years, Alex was involved in a serious accident that left him with a devastating knee injury. The doctors told him that he may never be able to walk again first, let alone compete in taekwondo. This news could have shattered his spirit and caused him to give up on his dreams. However, Alex refused to succumb to despair. He spent countless hours in physical therapy, pushing himself to regain strength and mobility in his injured knee. His unwavering determination and perseverance eventually paid off, and he was able to resume his training and compete once again.

Not long after his recovery, Alex suffered another setback when his family faced financial hardship. He was forced to work long hours to support his family, leaving him with little time and energy for training. Despite the immense pressure and challenges he was facing, Alex remained dedicated to his goal of reaching the Olympics. He continued to train whenever he could, sometimes in the early hours of the morning or late at night, refusing to let his circumstances dictate his future.

Finally, after years of hard work and sacrifice, Alex's determination and resilience paid off. He qualified for the Olympics, representing his country on the world stage and fulfilling his lifelong dream. His journey from adversity to success serves as an inspiration to athletes everywhere, proving that with unwavering determination and perseverance, any obstacle can be overcome.

Alex's story is a testament to the power of the human spirit and the resilience of the human mind. His refusal to give up in the face of adversity serves as a reminder that with hard work and dedication, anything is possible. His journey to the Olympics is a true triumph through taekwondo, and his inspirational tale will continue to inspire aspiring athletes for years to come.

~ Analysis of the importance of resilience and determination in the world of elite sports

In the world of elite sports, resilience and determination are of paramount importance. Athletes who excel at the highest levels of competition must possess an extraordinary level of mental fortitude to cope with the physical and emotional demands of their chosen discipline. This is particularly true in the sport of taekwondo, where competitors must demonstrate incredible strength, agility, and mental focus in order to succeed.

Resilience is the ability to bounce back from setbacks, to overcome adversity and thrive in the face of challenges. In the context of elite sports, resilience is often the difference between success and failure. Athletes who are able to maintain their composure and focus in the face of adversity are more likely to perform at their best, even under the most intense pressure.

Determination is equally essential. In order to excel in elite sports, athletes must be willing to push themselves to the absolute limit of their physical and mental capacities. This often requires an unwavering determination to succeed, even in the face of seemingly insurmountable obstacles.

In the world of taekwondo, where the brutal physicality of the sport is matched only by its mental demands, resilience and determination are the essential ingredients for success. Athletes must be able to endure grueling training regimens, physical injury, and the merciless competition of the highest levels of the sport in order to achieve their Olympic dreams.

From the story of a young athlete who overcame a debilitating injury to become an Olympic champion, to the tale of a competitor who faced seemingly insurmountable odds to reach the top of the podium, the book illustrates the extraordinary mental strength and unwavering determination that is required to succeed in the world of elite sports.

These stories serve as powerful reminders of the importance of resilience and determination in the pursuit of athletic excellence. They also highlight the profound impact that these qualities can have on an athlete's ability to overcome adversity and achieve greatness. As such, "Triumph through Taekwondo" stands as a testament to the power of the human spirit, and an inspiration to anyone who aspires to achieve their dreams, no matter the obstacles they may face.

Chapter 4: Overcoming Adversity

In this section of Triumph through Taekwondo, we delve into the stories of athletes who have faced and overcome significant adversity on their journey to achieving their Olympic dreams through the discipline of taekwondo.

One such athlete is Sarah, who overcame a serious injury to continue pursuing her taekwondo goals. Sarah's knee injury sidelined her for over a year, and she faced the challenge of not only physical rehabilitation, but also mental and emotional hurdles. Through unwavering determination and the support of her coaches and teammates, Sarah was able to overcome her adversity and return to the sport she loved. Her resilience and perseverance are a testament to the power of the human spirit in the face of adversity.

Another inspiring story is that of Diego, who grew up in a rough neighborhood and faced numerous obstacles on his path to becoming a taekwondo champion. Despite the constant pressure and temptation to fall into a life of crime and violence, Diego found solace and purpose in the discipline and training of taekwondo. Through his hard work and dedication, he was able to rise above his circumstances and achieve success in the sport. Diego's story illustrates the transformative power of taekwondo in overcoming adversity and building a positive life, even in the face of overwhelming challenges.

These stories, among others, highlight the common theme of perseverance, resilience, and determination in the face of adversity. They serve as a source of inspiration for anyone facing their own struggles, showing that with a strong will and the right support, it is possible to overcome even the most daunting obstacles.

Through their experiences, these athletes exemplify the true spirit of taekwondo, demonstrating that the discipline goes far beyond physical strength and skill. It is a way of life that instills important values such as perseverance, resilience, and determination, which are essential for overcoming adversity in any pursuit.

Join us as we explore these incredible stories of triumph over adversity and gain insight into the powerful impact of taekwondo in the lives of these athletes. Their journeys serve as a testament to the indomitable human spirit and the capacity for growth and transformation in the face of adversity.

~ Exploration of the various obstacles that athletes have had to conquer on their path to Olympic glory

The journey to Olympic glory is often a tumultuous one, filled with a myriad of obstacles that athletes must overcome in order to achieve their dreams. In the world of Taekwondo, this journey is particularly arduous, as athletes must navigate not only the physical demands of their sport, but also the mental and emotional challenges that come with competing at the highest level.

One of the most common obstacles that athletes face on their path to Olympic glory is injury. Taekwondo is an intense and physically demanding sport, and as a result, athletes are prone to a wide range of injuries, from minor strains and sprains to more serious ligament and bone injuries. These injuries can be devastating to an athlete's Olympic dreams, forcing them to undergo grueling rehabilitation and potentially sidelining them for months or even years at a time.

In addition to injury, athletes must also contend with the immense pressure and mental strain that comes with competing at the Olympics. The mental game of sports is often overlooked, but it is a crucial component of an athlete's success. Athletes must learn to navigate the high stakes, intense competition, and overwhelming pressure that come with performing on the world stage.

Furthermore, many athletes also have to overcome financial obstacles on their path to Olympic glory. Training at an elite level is incredibly expensive, and many athletes struggle to find the financial support they need to pursue their Olympic dreams. Without the necessary funding, athletes may find themselves unable to afford top-notch coaching, training facilities, and necessary equipment, making it all the more challenging to compete at the highest level.

Finally, athletes also face personal and emotional obstacles on their journey to Olympic glory. Many athletes come from difficult backgrounds, and have had to overcome significant adversity in order to pursue their dreams. Whether it is family or personal challenges, athletes often have to find a way to overcome these obstacles in order to achieve their Olympic goals.

Despite these obstacles, many athletes have triumphed through Taekwondo and achieved Olympic glory. Their stories are inspiring and serve as testament to the resilience, determination, and passion of these athletes. From overcoming injury and financial hardship to navigating the mental and emotional challenges of the sport, these athletes have proven that anything is possible with dedication and hard work.

These stories are a testament to the power of perseverance and the human spirit, and are sure to inspire readers of all ages.

~ Insight into the strategies and mindset needed to overcome adversity in the pursuit of one's goals

In the pursuit of achieving one's goals, whether they be in the realm of sports, academics, or personal development, obstacles and adversity are inevitable. However, it is often said that it is not the obstacles themselves but one's response to them that determines their ultimate success. This rings especially true in the sport of Taekwondo, where athletes face numerous physical, mental, and emotional challenges in their quest for excellence.

Through a series of compelling and uplifting stories, the book showcases the journeys of Taekwondo athletes who have faced and conquered various obstacles on their paths to realizing their Olympic dreams.

One of the key themes that emerges from these stories is the importance of resilience and perseverance in the face of adversity. Many of the athletes featured in the book have had to overcome significant obstacles, such as injuries, financial hardship, and personal setbacks. Yet, through their unwavering determination and positive mindset, they were able to push through these challenges and emerge stronger and more determined than ever.

Another crucial aspect highlighted in the book is the role of goal-setting and strategic planning in overcoming adversity. The athletes profiled in Triumph through Taekwondo demonstrate the power of setting clear, realistic goals and devising actionable plans to achieve them. Whether it is navigating the complexities of training and competition schedules, or overcoming self-doubt and setbacks, these athletes have shown that a well-defined plan and a strong sense of purpose can help conquer even the most daunting of obstacles.

Furthermore, the book sheds light on the significance of a strong support network in surmounting adversity. Behind every successful athlete in the book is a team of coaches, mentors, family members, and friends who have offered unwavering support and encouragement. Their role in providing emotional and practical assistance to the athletes in times of difficulty is not to be underestimated. .

Ultimately, Triumph through Taekwondo serves as a powerful testament to the inspirational stories of resilience, determination, and triumph in the face of adversity. It offers invaluable insights into the strategies and mindset needed to overcome obstacles on the journey to achieving one's goals, not just in Taekwondo, but in any pursuit in life. Whether you are an athlete yourself or simply someone in need of motivation and guidance, this book is sure to inspire and empower you on your own path to success.

Chapter 5: The Role of Mentors

Mentorship is a fundamental aspect of success in any discipline, and in the world of Taekwondo, the role of mentors is crucial in guiding athletes towards achieving their Olympic dreams. In this chapter, we will explore the stories of several Taekwondo athletes who have triumphed over obstacles with the help of their mentors.

Mentors play a significant role in the development of athletes, providing guidance, support, wisdom, and a roadmap to success. They are often experienced coaches, former athletes, or trusted individuals who have themselves excelled in the sport. Their influence goes beyond mere technical instruction; they serve as role models and sources of inspiration, instilling the values of discipline, perseverance, and dedication in their protégés.

One such example is the story of Sarah, a talented young Taekwondo athlete who faced numerous challenges on her path to achieving her Olympic dream. Sarah's mentor, a former Olympic medalist, took her under his wing and became not only her coach but also her confidant and source of motivation. With his guidance, Sarah was able to overcome self-doubt, develop a winning mindset, and eventually, secured a spot on the national team, setting her on the path to Olympic glory.

Another compelling story is that of David, a Taekwondo athlete who struggled with a debilitating injury that threatened to end his career. Through the unwavering support and encouragement of his mentor, a respected coach with years of experience, David was able to overcome his physical limitations, regain his strength, and make a remarkable comeback. His mentor's belief in him during his darkest moments proved to be the catalyst for David's resurgence, ultimately propelling him to Olympic triumph.

These stories demonstrate the indispensable role that mentors play in the lives of Taekwondo athletes. Their guidance and unwavering support not only serve to refine technique and physical prowess but also to cultivate the mental fortitude and resilience necessary to surmount obstacles and achieve greatness.

Mentorship is a reciprocal relationship; while mentors provide invaluable guidance and support, athletes also have the opportunity to learn and grow from the wealth of knowledge and experience that their mentors impart. The bond forged between mentor and athlete serves as a source of strength and inspiration, empowering athletes to push beyond their limits and strive for excellence.

The stories of perseverance and triumph in this chapter bear testament to the profound impact of mentorship, underscoring its crucial role in transforming aspiring athletes into victorious Olympians.

- Accounts of athletes who credit their coaches and mentors for helping them achieve success in Taekwondo

One such athlete is Mia, who started practicing Taekwondo at the age of 8. She showed immense potential from the very beginning and was quickly recognized as a rising star in the sport. However, it was not until she met her coach, Master Kim, that Mia truly began to develop into the elite athlete that she is today.

Master Kim was not only a skilled Taekwondo practitioner himself, but he also had a deep understanding of the mental and emotional aspects of the sport. He knew how to push Mia to her limits without breaking her spirit, and how to hone her strengths while working on her weaknesses. Under his guidance, Mia went on to win numerous national and international competitions, eventually earning a spot on the Olympic team.

In her interviews, Mia always credits Master Kim for her success, saying that she would never have achieved her dreams without his mentorship and support. She describes how he instilled in her a sense of discipline, dedication, and perseverance, not only in Taekwondo but in all aspects of her life.

Similarly, another athlete, Zach, has a remarkable story of overcoming adversity with the help of his coach, Coach Lee. Zach came from a troubled background and had a history of getting into trouble. It wasn't until he started practicing Taekwondo under the guidance of Coach Lee that he began to turn his life around.

Coach Lee saw enormous potential in Zach and took him under his wing, providing him with the guidance and support that he so desperately needed. Through Taekwondo, Zach learned the value of hard work, respect, and self-discipline. With Coach Lee's mentorship, Zach went on to become a national champion and eventually earned a spot on the Olympic team.

In interviews, Zach always talks about how Coach Lee believed in him even when he didn't believe in himself, and how his coach's unwavering support and guidance played a crucial role in shaping him into the athlete and the person that he is today.

These stories, and many others like them, serve as a testament to the powerful impact that coaches and mentors can have on athletes' lives. Through their dedication, wisdom, and support, they not only help athletes achieve success in their sport but also shape them into resilient, disciplined, and empowered individuals.

Triumph Through Taekwondo is filled with such inspirational stories of athletes who have overcome various obstacles with the help of their coaches and mentors. It highlights the transformative power of Taekwondo and the crucial role that coaches and mentors play in the success of athletes. These accounts serve as a reminder of the importance of mentorship and support in the journey towards achieving Olympic dreams.

~ Examination of the impact of mentorship on athletes' performance and mindset

When examining the impact of mentorship on athletes' performance and mindset, it is important to consider the role that mentors play in guiding and supporting athletes as they strive to achieve their Olympic dreams.

Mentors can provide athletes with valuable knowledge, experience, and perspective that can help them navigate the often challenging and competitive world of sports. They can offer guidance on technical skills, mental toughness, and the overall mindset needed to excel in their sport. This guidance can be particularly important for athletes who come from underprivileged backgrounds or face obstacles such as discrimination, lack of resources, or personal struggles.

For example, in the book Triumph through Taekwondo, a young athlete from a low-income community shares how a mentor not only coached her in the physical aspects of taekwondo but also provided guidance on navigating social and economic challenges. This mentorship helped her develop the resilience and determination needed to pursue her Olympic dreams despite the odds stacked against her.

Furthermore, mentors can serve as role models and sources of inspiration for athletes. By sharing their own experiences and lessons learned, mentors can motivate athletes to push beyond their limits and strive for excellence. This kind of positive influence can be invaluable for athletes who may be facing self-doubt, fear of failure, or other mental barriers that can hinder their performance.

In the book, Triumph through Taekwondo, numerous athletes credit their mentors with instilling in them a strong work ethic, a growth mindset, and the ability to overcome setbacks. They describe how their mentors' support and encouragement helped them stay focused and motivated, especially during times of injury, defeat, or adversity.

In summary, mentorship plays a crucial role in shaping athletes' performance and mindset. The stories shared in Triumph through Taekwondo offer compelling evidence of how mentorship can make a significant difference in the lives and careers of athletes, enabling them to overcome obstacles and achieve their Olympic dreams. As such, the impact of mentorship on athletes' success is a vital aspect of sports development and should be given the attention it deserves.

Chapter 6: The Road to Redemption

This section of the book is particularly inspiring as it delves into the depths of the human spirit and the resilience of these athletes as they faced and overcame adversity.

One such athlete is Sarah, who had a promising taekwondo career derailed by a series of injuries and setbacks. After feeling like her dream of competing at the Olympics was slipping away, Sarah found the strength within herself to pick herself up and continue pursuing her passion. Through hard work, determination, and unwavering dedication to her sport, Sarah was able to overcome her injuries and make a triumphant return to competition.

Similarly, we also meet Chris, whose personal struggles and self-doubt threatened to derail his taekwondo career. Facing challenges both on and off the mat, Chris found himself spiraling into a dark place, unsure if he would ever be able to regain the focus and drive that once propelled him towards his Olympic goals. However, through the support of his coaches, teammates, and his own inner resolve, Chris was able to confront his demons and make a stunning comeback, ultimately achieving his dream of representing his country on the Olympic stage.

The stories of Sarah and Chris, along with many others featured in this chapter, serve as powerful reminders of the resilience of the human spirit and the capacity for individuals to overcome even the most daunting challenges. Their journeys toward redemption are a testament to the transformative power of sport and the incredible impact it can have on our lives.

Readers will find themselves deeply moved and inspired by the triumphs of these athletes as they navigate the highs and lows of their taekwondo careers. Through their stories, we are reminded of the importance of perseverance, belief in oneself, and the unwavering commitment to one's goals, no matter how difficult the path may seem.

These stories will leave readers feeling inspired and motivated to overcome their own challenges, both on and off the mat.

~ Stories of athletes who faced setbacks and failures but ultimately found redemption through their dedication to Taekwondo

The world of Taekwondo is filled with stories of athletes who have faced setbacks and failures but ultimately found redemption through their dedication to the sport.

One such athlete is Yuna Kim, a South Korean Taekwondo practitioner who experienced a series of setbacks early in her career. As a young athlete, Yuna struggled with self-doubt and lacked confidence in her abilities. Despite her natural talent and relentless training, she often found herself defeated in competitions, leading her to question whether she had what it takes to succeed in the sport.

However, with the guidance of her coaches and the support of her family, Yuna refused to give up. She continued to train tirelessly, focusing on improving her skills and cultivating a winning mindset. Her dedication eventually paid off when she earned a spot on the South Korean national Taekwondo team. With newfound confidence, Yuna went on to compete in numerous international tournaments, eventually earning a gold medal at the Olympics.

Another athlete featured in the book is Javier Martinez, a Mexican Taekwondo practitioner who faced financial struggles in his pursuit of Olympic glory. Growing up in a low-income neighborhood, Javier's family could not afford to support his Taekwondo training. Undeterred, Javier took odd jobs and sought sponsors to cover the costs of his coaching, equipment, and travel expenses.

Despite his financial hardships, Javier remained committed to his dream of representing Mexico at the Olympics. He trained relentlessly, often sacrificing personal comforts and leisure time to pursue his goals. His perseverance paid off when he qualified for the Olympic team and earned a bronze medal in the Taekwondo competition.

These stories, along with many others in the book, serve as powerful reminders of the resilience and determination of Taekwondo athletes. They inspire readers to overcome their own challenges, push through setbacks, and strive for greatness in their own pursuits.

Through their dedication, these athletes have not only achieved their Olympic dreams but have also become role models for others, demonstrating the transformative power of perseverance and resilience. Triumph through Taekwondo offers a compelling look at the human spirit and the incredible feats that can be accomplished through unwavering dedication to a passion.

~ Analysis of how resilience and perseverance can lead to ultimate triumph in the face of defeat

The book is a collection of stories of taekwondo athletes who have faced numerous obstacles on their path to achieving their Olympic dreams, and how they have overcome these challenges through their resilience and perseverance.

One of the key aspects of resilience and perseverance that the book explores is the ability of athletes to bounce back from adversity. Many of the athletes featured in the book have faced setbacks such as injuries, financial struggles, and personal hardships, yet they have continued to push forward and pursue their dreams. Their ability to overcome these obstacles demonstrates the resilience and determination that has ultimately led to their triumph.

Additionally, the book delves into the importance of never giving up, even in the face of seemingly insurmountable challenges. The athletes' stories illustrate how they have refused to succumb to defeat, even when the odds were stacked against them. This unwavering determination has been a driving force behind their ability to ultimately achieve success in their athletic pursuits.

Moreover, the book also highlights the role of perseverance in the athletes' journeys. It depicts how they have remained committed to their goals, despite the numerous hardships they have encountered along the way. Their persistence in the face of adversity serves as an important lesson in the power of perseverance in overcoming obstacles and achieving success.

Furthermore, "Triumph through Taekwondo" underscores the transformative nature of resilience and perseverance. The athletes' experiences demonstrate how they have grown and developed as individuals through their struggles, ultimately emerging stronger and more determined to succeed. This transformative process has been essential in enabling them to triumph over their setbacks and emerge victorious in their pursuit of Olympic dreams.

Overall, "Triumph through Taekwondo" provides powerful insights into how resilience and perseverance can lead to ultimate triumph in the face of defeat. Through the stories of these remarkable athletes, the book serves as an inspiring testament to the transformative power of determination and the resilience of the human spirit. It offers invaluable lessons not only for aspiring athletes but for anyone facing challenges in their own pursuit of success.

Chapter 7: Sacrifice and Discipline

I takes readers on a journey through the lives of several taekwondo athletes who have faced difficult challenges and made significant sacrifices in order to achieve success in the sport.

The chapter begins by introducing readers to the world of taekwondo, providing a brief overview of its history, as well as its modern Olympic status. From there, i delves into the personal stories of the athletes, highlighting the incredible level of discipline and dedication they have shown in the pursuit of their goals.

One such story is that of Sarah, a young athlete who grew up in a small town, where she faced adversity and discrimination due to her gender. Despite the obstacles, she was determined to pursue her passion for taekwondo. The chapter reveals the sacrifices Sarah made, including moving away from her family and training for countless hours each day, all in the pursuit of her Olympic dream.

I also explores the role of discipline in the lives of these athletes, highlighting the grueling training regimens they must adhere to in order to compete at an elite level. Readers are given a firsthand look at the physical and mental toll that this level of training can take on an individual, as well as the mental fortitude required to push through the pain and exhaustion.

As the chapter progresses, i draws parallels between the sacrifices and discipline required in taekwondo and the broader concept of overcoming obstacles in pursuit of any ambitious goal. The stories of these athletes serve as a powerful reminder that success rarely comes without sacrifice and disciplined effort - whether in taekwondo or any other endeavor.

It serves as a testament to the resilience and determination of the human spirit, and the power of sacrifice and discipline in the pursuit of excellence. As readers follow these athletes' journeys, they will be motivated to push through their own obstacles, knowing that sacrifice and discipline are essential to reaching their own triumphs.

- Examples of athletes who made sacrifices and maintained strict discipline in order to reach the pinnacle of their sport

1. Steven Lopez- Steven Lopez is a legendary Taekwondo athlete who has won numerous Olympic medals and World Championships. His journey to success was not easy, as he had to overcome financial difficulties and family expectations. Steven and his siblings trained hard in Taekwondo, often sacrificing their social lives and other opportunities to focus on their sport. Their dedication and discipline paid off when Steven achieved his Olympic dream, proving that sacrifices and strict training are essential in reaching the pinnacle of Taekwondo.

2. Jade Jones- Jade Jones is a British Taekwondo athlete who became the youngest Olympic champion in her sport at the age of 19. Her path to success was paved with sacrifices, as she had to dedicate herself to intensive training and strict discipline. Jade's tenacity and determination paid off when she

won two Olympic gold medals, showcasing her incredible talent and commitment to her sport.

3. Hadi Saei- Hadi Saei is an Iranian Taekwondo athlete who has achieved remarkable success in his career, winning multiple Olympic medals and World Championships. Hadi's journey was filled with sacrifices, as he had to endure grueling training sessions and strict discipline to excel in his sport. Despite facing cultural and political challenges, Hadi's unwavering dedication and sacrifices ultimately led him to become one of the greatest Taekwondo athletes of all time.

4. Kimia Alizadeh- Kimia Alizadeh made history as the first Iranian Taekwondo athlete to win an Olympic medal, a bronze, at the 2016 Rio Olympics. She faced numerous challenges and sacrifices, including having to train in an environment where women's sports were not widely supported. Kimia's perseverance and unwavering commitment allowed her to excel in her sport and make a lasting impact on Taekwondo.

5. Aaron Cook- Aaron Cook is a British Taekwondo athlete who had to overcome significant obstacles and make sacrifices to achieve success in his sport. He faced internal conflict within the national team and made the difficult decision to train independently, sacrificing support and resources to pursue his Olympic dreams. Aaron's dedication and resilience

led him to become a World Champion and a force to be reckoned with in Taekwondo.

These athletes' stories exemplify the sacrifices and discipline required to reach the pinnacle of Taekwondo and achieve Olympic dreams. Their unwavering commitment and relentless pursuit of excellence serve as an inspiration to aspiring athletes and showcase the power of triumph through Taekwondo.

- Exploration of the role of sacrifice and discipline in achieving Olympic dreams

Sacrifice and discipline are two key components in the pursuit of any Olympic dream. For athletes in the world of taekwondo, these elements are particularly vital as they navigate the rigorous training, competition, and personal challenges that come with working towards the pinnacle of their sport.

The journey to becoming an Olympic taekwondo athlete is incredibly demanding, both physically and mentally. Athletes must commit to long hours of training, often sacrificing social events and personal time in order to pursue their goals. This level of dedication requires discipline and a strong sense of purpose, as athletes must stay focused on their training regimen and continually push themselves to improve.

Many Olympic hopefuls have had to make significant sacrifices in order to pursue their dreams. This can include relocating to train with the best coaches and training partners, giving up financial stability to focus on their athletic career, or even sacrificing personal relationships in order to fully commit to their training. These sacrifices can take a toll on athletes, but those who are able to persevere and maintain their discipline are often the ones who find success in reaching their Olympic dreams.

Discipline is also crucial in terms of the daily grind of training. Athletes must adhere to strict routines, including conditioning, technical training, sparring, and mental preparation. This often requires early morning wake-up calls, disciplined diets, and the ability to push through physical and mental fatigue. For Olympic level taekwondo athletes, discipline is not just a choice, but a necessity if they hope to compete at the highest level.

The stories of Olympic taekwondo athletes are filled with tales of sacrifice and discipline. From overcoming injuries and setbacks to fighting through personal hardships, these athletes exemplify the spirit of perseverance. Their dedication to their sport and their unwavering discipline in the face of adversity serves as an inspiration to anyone striving to achieve their own goals.

Through their stories, readers will see the incredible resilience and determination required to achieve greatness in the sport of taekwondo, and find inspiration to apply these values to their own pursuits.

Ultimately, the exploration of sacrifice and discipline in the context of Olympic taekwondo serves as a testament to the power of unwavering determination and the ability to overcome obstacles in the relentless pursuit of one's dreams. These qualities not only lead to success in the athletic arena but also serve as valuable lessons for leading a fulfilling and purpose-driven life.

Chapter 8: Celebrating Diversity

This chapter delves into the stories of athletes who have overcome various obstacles to achieve their Olympic dreams, highlighting the significance of diversity and the positive impact it has on the sport.

The chapter begins by exploring the global nature of taekwondo, which has roots in Korea but has spread to numerous countries around the world. This widespread popularity has allowed individuals from diverse backgrounds to participate in the sport, contributing to its rich tapestry of cultures and traditions.

One of the central themes of this chapter is the power of representation. By showcasing athletes from different ethnicities, genders, and socioeconomic backgrounds, taekwondo has become a beacon of diversity and inclusivity. Through the personal narratives of these athletes, readers gain insight into the unique challenges they have faced and the ways in which they have triumphed over adversity.

The chapter also examines the profound impact of diversity on the overall development of taekwondo as a sport. By embracing different perspectives and experiences, athletes have been able to enrich the discipline with new ideas, training techniques, and innovative approaches to competition. Through their dedication and perseverance, they have shattered stereotypes and redefined what it means to be a taekwondo athlete.

Furthermore, the chapter delves into the social and cultural significance of embracing diversity in sports. It highlights the importance of creating a welcoming and inclusive environment within taekwondo communities, where athletes feel valued and supported regardless of their background. By doing so, the sport has the potential to make a meaningful and lasting impact on individuals and society as a whole.

Through the inspiring stories of athletes who have defied the odds and overcome barriers, readers are reminded of the profound impact that inclusivity and representation can have on the sport and the world at large. Triumph through Taekwondo celebrates the importance of diversity and serves as a testament to the remarkable achievements that can result from embracing and honoring the unique qualities of all individuals.

- Highlighting the diverse backgrounds and journeys of athletes in the world of Taekwondo

Taekwondo is a martial art that is known for its impressive athleticism and agility, but behind the powerful kicks and graceful movements, there are also incredible stories of perseverance and triumph. In the world of Taekwondo, athletes come from diverse backgrounds and have faced a wide range of challenges on their journey to success.

One of the most fascinating aspects of Taekwondo is the wide range of backgrounds from which athletes hail. Some have grown up in the tradition of their families, with Taekwondo running through their veins from a young age. Others have stumbled upon the sport later in life, and have had to backtrack to catch up to their peers who started much earlier.

For example, there are athletes who have been training in Taekwondo since childhood, learning the strikes and forms as soon as they could walk. These individuals often have a deep-seated passion for the sport and have spent years perfecting their skills. Their journey has been one of growth and dedication to their craft, often in the face of doubt and skepticism from those who didn't understand their goals.

On the other hand, there are athletes who may not have discovered Taekwondo until their teenage or adult years, but quickly fell in love with the sport and dedicated themselves to mastering it. These individuals have had to work tirelessly to catch up to their peers who started much earlier in life, but their determination and drive have propelled them to great achievements.

In addition to the diverse backgrounds of athletes in Taekwondo, their journeys to success are often marked by overcoming obstacles. Some have faced financial difficulties, struggling to afford quality training or competition opportunities. Others have dealt with injuries that threatened to derail their dreams, but refused to let setbacks define them. There are also those who have had to navigate societal expectations and stereotypes, breaking down barriers and proving that they belong in the world of Taekwondo.

These stories of resilience and determination are a testament to the strength of the human spirit, and serve as an inspiration to all who have faced their own obstacles.

Through their passion for Taekwondo, these athletes have found a way to rise above adversity and achieve their Olympic dreams.

Their stories serve as a reminder that success in Taekwondo, and in life, is not only about physical prowess, but also about the strength of the mind and the indomitable will to never give up.

~ Examination of how diversity adds richness and depth to the sport of Taekwondo

Diversity is a key component of what makes the sport of Taekwondo so rich and vibrant. In fact, one could argue that without diversity, the sport would not be what it is today. When we talk about diversity in Taekwondo, we are referring to a wide range of factors, including ethnic and cultural diversity, as well as diversity in terms of age, gender, and physical ability.

One of the most obvious ways in which diversity adds richness and depth to Taekwondo is through the variety of martial arts styles and techniques that are brought to the sport by athletes from different cultural backgrounds. Taekwondo itself is a Korean martial art, but it has been heavily influenced by other martial arts from around the world, including Chinese, Japanese, and Southeast Asian martial arts. As a result, Taekwondo has evolved into a truly global and diverse sport, with athletes from all corners of the globe bringing their own unique styles and techniques to the mat.

This diversity in martial arts styles and techniques not only makes Taekwondo an exciting and dynamic sport to watch, but it also encourages innovation and creativity among athletes. When athletes from different backgrounds come together to train and compete, they are exposed to new ideas and perspectives, which often leads to the development of new and innovative techniques that benefit the entire Taekwondo community.

Furthermore, diversity in Taekwondo extends beyond the mat and into the broader global community. As the sport continues to grow in popularity around the world, athletes from diverse ethnic and cultural backgrounds are being given the opportunity to represent their countries on the international stage. This not only promotes cultural exchange and understanding, but it also serves as a powerful symbol of unity and solidarity among nations.

In addition to cultural diversity, Taekwondo also demonstrates diversity in terms of age, gender, and physical ability. Unlike some sports, Taekwondo is truly open to individuals of all ages and abilities. From young children to senior citizens, and from able-bodied athletes to those with disabilities, Taekwondo offers something for everyone.

The inclusion of athletes from diverse age groups, genders, and physical abilities brings richness and depth to the sport in a variety of ways. It fosters a sense of community and inclusivity, and it helps to break down stereotypes and misconceptions about who can and cannot participate in Taekwondo. Furthermore, it provides role models for individuals who may feel underrepresented in the sport, and it serves as a reminder that everyone has the potential to achieve greatness through Taekwondo, regardless of their background or circumstances.

Ultimately, the diversity of Taekwondo is what makes the sport so special and unique. It is a sport that celebrates and embraces the wealth of human experience and capability, and as a result, it is constantly evolving and growing in exciting new ways. Whether it's through the fusion of martial arts styles, the global representation of athletes, or the inclusivity of individuals from all walks of life, diversity adds immeasurable richness and depth to the sport of Taekwondo.

Chapter 9: Strength Through Unity

In the world of Taekwondo, there is a strong emphasis on unity and working together as a team. This sense of togetherness and collective strength is not only evident within the sport itself, but also in the personal lives of the athletes who practice it. In this chapter, we will delve into the stories of individuals who have found strength through unity, both on and off the mat, as they overcome obstacles to achieve their Olympic dreams.

One such athlete is Maria, a Taekwondo practitioner from a small town in Brazil. Maria grew up in a financially disadvantaged neighborhood, where gang violence and crime were prevalent. Despite the challenges she faced, Maria found solace and support in her Taekwondo community. Her training partners and instructors became like family to her, providing her with the strength and encouragement she needed to pursue her athletic goals. Through their collective support, Maria was able to rise above her circumstances and eventually represented her country on the Olympic stage.

Similarly, in South Korea, a country known for its dominance in the sport of Taekwondo, we meet Tae-jun, a young athlete with a passion for the martial art. Tae-jun was born with a physical disability that made it difficult for him to compete at the same level as his able-bodied counterparts. However, through the support of his coaches and training partners, Tae-jun was able to overcome his limitations and excel in the sport. The sense of unity and camaraderie within his Taekwondo community enabled him to push past his physical boundaries and achieve his Olympic dreams.

These stories highlight the importance of unity in the world of Taekwondo. Beyond the physical demands of the sport, it is the sense of togetherness and solidarity that propels athletes to success. Whether it is through the support of training partners, coaches, or the larger Taekwondo community, the strength that comes from unity is undeniable.

The athletes featured in this chapter found their strength through unity, drawing on the support and encouragement of their peers to overcome obstacles and achieve their Olympic dreams. Their stories serve as a powerful reminder of the transformative power of community and the unbreakable bond that is forged through the practice of Taekwondo.

- Accounts of athletes who found strength and unity through teamwork and camaraderie in Taekwondo

Triumph through Taekwondo is a collection of inspiring stories of athletes who have overcome various obstacles to achieve their Olympic dreams. One common theme running through these accounts is the strength and unity that comes from teamwork and camaraderie in Taekwondo.

One such story is that of Sarah, a young athlete who found herself battling with self-doubt and lack of confidence. At her lowest point, she was ready to give up on her dreams of becoming an Olympic Taekwondo champion. It wasn't until she joined a team of like-minded individuals that she began to find the support and encouragement she needed to push through her self-imposed limitations. Through the strength and unity of her teammates, Sarah was able to overcome her fears and go on to compete at the highest levels of Taekwondo.

Similarly, the story of Kyle, a promising athlete who faced personal challenges and setbacks, illustrates the power of teamwork and camaraderie in Taekwondo. After suffering a serious injury that threatened to derail his Olympic dreams, Kyle was faced with the daunting task of rehabilitation and regaining his physical strength. It was through the support of his teammates and coaches that Kyle was able to find the motivation and determination to push through his recovery and eventually make a triumphant return to the sport.

These are just a few examples of the many athletes who have found strength and unity through teamwork and camaraderie in Taekwondo. The bonds formed in the pursuit of their Olympic dreams have not only helped them overcome personal struggles, but have also created a sense of belonging and community that extends beyond the confines of the sport.

Triumph through Taekwondo captures these powerful stories of resilience and determination, showcasing the transformative power of teamwork and camaraderie in the lives of these athletes. Their accounts serve as an inspiration to anyone facing their own challenges, demonstrating that with the support of others, anything is possible. The book is a testament to the strength and unity that can be found in the pursuit of a common goal, and a celebration of the human spirit's ability to triumph over adversity.

- Discussion of how teamwork and collaboration can enhance individual and team performance

Taekwondo is a martial art that emphasizes discipline, self-control, and respect for others. Practitioners of taekwondo often use teamwork and collaboration to achieve their goals, whether it's in the studio or competing in national or international competitions.

Teamwork and collaboration are essential components of taekwondo training. In order to excel in this martial art, individuals must work together to accomplish their goals. This is especially true in sparring, where practitioners engage in simulated combat to improve their skills. Through teamwork and collaboration, individuals can push each other to their limits, striving to become the best martial artists they can be.

Teamwork and collaboration can also enhance individual performance by providing support and encouragement. In taekwondo, practitioners often train with a group of peers who can offer motivation and guidance. By working together, individuals can learn from each other's strengths and weaknesses, pushing each other to improve and reach new levels of achievement. This sense of camaraderie can be a powerful motivator, leading to increased individual performance.

On a team level, teamwork and collaboration can lead to improved performance by creating a sense of unity and shared purpose. In taekwondo competitions, teams rely on each other to achieve success. By working together, teammates can help each other overcome obstacles and improve their overall performance. This collaborative effort can create a strong sense of community and pride, leading to enhanced team performance.

Overall, the discussion of teamwork and collaboration in Triumph through Taekwondo highlights their significance in maximizing individual and team performance. Through teamwork and collaboration, individuals can strive for excellence in their martial arts practice, while also fostering a strong sense of camaraderie and support within their team. This can ultimately lead to achieving Olympic dreams and overcoming a range of obstacles along the way.

Chapter 10: Adaptability and Innovation

This chapter delves into the ways in which athletes in this sport must continuously adapt to new challenges, situations, and opponents, as well as innovate in their training methods and techniques in order to succeed at the highest levels.

The chapter highlights the stories of several taekwondo athletes who have triumphed in the face of adversity through their ability to adapt and innovate. One such athlete is a young competitor who, after suffering a devastating injury, had to completely rework her training regimen and adjust her technique in order to continue pursuing her Olympic dreams. Through sheer determination and an open-minded approach to change, she was able to adapt to her new physical limitations and innovate her training routine to ultimately achieve success on the international stage.

Another story featured in this chapter is that of a veteran taekwondo competitor who, nearing the end of his career, found himself in need of a fresh approach to training in order to remain competitive. Embracing the concept of adaptability, he sought out new coaching methods and training partners, ultimately finding a renewed sense of purpose and drive that propelled him to new heights in his sport.

Throughout the chapter, the book explores the ways in which these athletes embodied the principles of adaptability and innovation, and how their perseverance in the face of challenges serves as an inspiration to others. It also offers insights into the broader implications of these principles, emphasizing the importance of being open to change and constantly seeking new ways to push the boundaries of what is possible in taekwondo and beyond.

In addition to the individual stories, the chapter also delves into the broader impact that adaptability and innovation have had on the sport of taekwondo as a whole. It discusses the ways in which advancements in technology, sports science, and training methods have fundamentally shifted the way athletes prepare for competitions, and the role that adaptability plays in staying ahead of the curve in a rapidly evolving sport.

Through captivating stories of perseverance and achievement, this chapter underscores the importance of these principles not only in athletic pursuits, but also as essential tools for navigating the challenges of life.

- Stories of athletes who have adapted to changing circumstances and embraced innovation to enhance their skills in Taekwondo

Athletes in the sport of Taekwondo are a unique breed, as they not only possess impressive physical skills, but they also have the mental toughness to overcome obstacles and adapt to changing circumstances.

One such athlete is Sarah, a Taekwondo practitioner who faced a devastating knee injury that threatened to derail her Olympic dreams. Instead of giving up, Sarah sought out the latest advancements in sports medicine and rehabilitation techniques to recover from her injury. She worked tirelessly to strengthen her knee and focused on refining her technique to compensate for any lingering limitations. Through sheer determination and a willingness to adapt, Sarah not only recovered from her injury but also became a stronger and more resilient athlete.

Another athlete, Alex, found himself at a crossroads in his Taekwondo career when he realized that his traditional training methods were no longer sufficient to compete at the highest level. Instead of clinging to outdated techniques, Alex embraced innovation by incorporating new training methods and technologies into his routine. He utilized video analysis to study and improve his form, and he experimented with new strength and conditioning exercises to enhance his physical abilities. By embracing innovation and adapting to the changing landscape of the sport, Alex was able to elevate his skills and compete at a level he never thought possible.

These stories, and many others in the book, illustrate the importance of adaptability and innovation in the world of Taekwondo. Athletes who are willing to embrace new ideas and technologies, and who are able to pivot in the face of adversity, are the ones who ultimately achieve their Olympic dreams. Whether it's overcoming a devastating injury, evolving training methods, or integrating cutting-edge technology, the athletes in "Triumph through Taekwondo" demonstrate that the ability to adapt and innovate is crucial for success in the sport.

These athletes have shown that by embracing change and seeking out new ways to enhance their skills, they can overcome any obstacle and achieve their dreams. Their stories inspire and motivate readers to approach their own challenges with a spirit of innovation and a willingness to adapt.

- Exploration of the importance of adaptability and innovation in staying ahead in a competitive sporting environment

In the competitive environment of modern day sports, staying ahead of the game is crucial in achieving success. Athletes and teams must constantly adapt and innovate to remain competitive and rise to the top of their respective sports. This is especially true in sports like taekwondo, where the landscape is constantly changing and evolving.

Adaptability is a key factor in success in sports, as athletes must be able to adjust to new strategies, techniques, and rules in their sport. This can be seen in the story of a taekwondo athlete who struggled with injuries, but embarked on a new training regimen that focused on flexibility and agility, ultimately leading to improved performance and success in competition.

Innovation is also crucial in staying ahead in a competitive sporting environment. Athletes and coaches must constantly seek new methods and technologies to gain a competitive edge. Whether it's a new training technique, a unique approach to mental preparation, or cutting-edge equipment, innovation is essential for reaching the top of the podium. In "Triumph through Taekwondo," readers will learn about how athletes and coaches have embraced innovation to achieve their goals, from using visualization techniques to improve performance to incorporating new technologies into training programs.

The book also explores the importance of a proactive and resilient mindset in the face of adversity. Athletes face numerous obstacles on their journey to success, and the ability to adapt and innovate in response to these challenges is critical. In "Triumph through Taekwondo," readers will find inspiring stories of athletes who overcame setbacks through creative problem-solving and determination.

By highlighting the experiences of athletes who have achieved success through adaptability, innovation, and resilience, "Triumph through Taekwondo" offers valuable lessons for individuals striving for excellence in the competitive world of sports. Whether you're a competitive athlete, a coach, or simply a sports enthusiast looking for inspiration, this book offers a powerful reminder of the importance of adaptability and innovation in reaching your goals. Through these stories, readers will gain insight into how to cultivate these essential qualities and apply them to their own athletic pursuits.

Chapter 11: Triumph of the Human Spirit

One such story is that of Maria, a taekwondo athlete from a small town in Colombia. Maria grew up in poverty and faced numerous obstacles in pursuing her passion for taekwondo. Despite the financial hardship and lack of resources, Maria never gave up on her dream of becoming an Olympic taekwondo champion. Through hard work, dedication, and unwavering perseverance, Maria overcame all the odds to qualify for the Olympic Games.

Another inspiring tale in this chapter is that of Ahmed, a Syrian refugee who found solace and purpose in taekwondo. Forced to flee his war-torn country, Ahmed faced the tremendous challenge of starting over in a new land with a different language and culture. Despite the immense adversity he faced, Ahmed channeled his resilience and determination into his taekwondo training. Through sheer willpower and a steadfast belief in his abilities, Ahmed went on to represent his new home at the Olympics, inspiring many with his incredible journey.

These stories, and many others shared in this chapter, exemplify the power of the human spirit to overcome seemingly insurmountable obstacles. The athletes featured in this section of the book demonstrate unwavering perseverance, unbreakable resolve, and an indomitable spirit, inspiring readers to never give up on their dreams, no matter the challenges they may face.

Furthermore, this chapter shines a light on the true essence of the Olympic spirit, where athletes from all walks of life come together to showcase the triumph of the human spirit in its purest form. Ultimately, the stories in this chapter serve as a reminder that with determination, resilience, and unwavering belief in oneself, anything is possible. The triumph of the human spirit knows no bounds, and these athletes are living testimony to that.

- Inspiring tales of athletes who have overcome physical and emotional obstacles to achieve their Olympic dreams through Taekwondo

Taekwondo is a martial art that demands physical strength, mental resilience, and unwavering discipline. For those who choose to pursue it as a sport, the journey is paved with obstacles that can seem insurmountable.

The stories in this book are a testament to the human spirit and the incredible power of perseverance. Each athlete faced their own unique set of obstacles, from physical injuries to personal tragedies, and yet they refused to let these challenges define them. Instead, they used their love for Taekwondo as a source of strength, pushing themselves beyond their limits to achieve their Olympic dreams.

One such athlete is Sarah, a promising young Taekwondo practitioner who suffered a devastating knee injury that threatened to derail her career. Instead of giving up, Sarah worked tirelessly to rehabilitate her knee, enduring countless hours of physical therapy and grueling workouts. Her dedication and determination paid off when she qualified for the Olympic team, proving that resilience and perseverance can triumph over adversity.

Another remarkable story is that of Jason, who overcame a troubled childhood to become a Taekwondo champion. Battling with anger and self-doubt, Jason found solace in the discipline and focus of Taekwondo. Through sheer determination, he transformed himself into a world-class athlete, using his experiences to inspire others facing similar hardships.

These stories not only showcase the physical prowess of these athletes, but also their unyielding spirit and inner strength. Their remarkable journeys serve as a reminder that with unwavering determination and relentless drive, any obstacle can be overcome.

Triumph through Taekwondo is a celebration of the indomitable human spirit and a testament to the power of perseverance. Through these inspiring tales, readers are invited to witness the resilience and fortitude of athletes who refused to be defined by their circumstances, choosing instead to defy the odds and achieve their Olympic dreams. Their stories are a source of inspiration for anyone facing challenges, proving that with passion, resilience, and unwavering determination, anything is possible.

- Examination of the enduring power of the human spirit in the face of adversity

These athletes have faced adversity in various forms, from physical disabilities to economic hardship, and have utilized the discipline and perseverance inherent in the sport of taekwondo to triumph over their obstacles.

One of the most enduring themes in Triumph through Taekwondo is the power of resilience in the face of adversity. The book illustrates how athletes have overcome physical and emotional adversities to achieve their Olympic dreams. Many of the athletes featured in the book have faced significant physical challenges, such as injuries or disabilities, that could have derailed their athletic aspirations. However, through their unwavering determination and the practice of taekwondo, they have been able to overcome these obstacles and achieve success in their sport.

In addition to physical challenges, Triumph through Taekwondo also underscores the impact of economic and social adversities on athletes. Many of the athletes in the book have come from underprivileged backgrounds, facing financial struggles and limited access to training and resources. Despite these challenges, they have demonstrated the power of the human spirit to persevere and achieve their goals. Through the practice of taekwondo, these athletes have found a sense of empowerment and fortitude that has propelled them to success.

Triumph through Taekwondo celebrates the ability of individuals to rise above their circumstances and pursue their dreams with unwavering determination and resilience. These athletes serve as inspiring examples of the enduring power of the human spirit in the face of adversity, demonstrating the transformative potential of taekwondo in overcoming life's challenges.

Overall, Triumph through Taekwondo brilliantly illustrates the incredible feats that can be achieved by individuals who embody the power of the human spirit. The book's portrayal of athletes overcoming physical, economic, and social challenges through the practice of taekwondo serves as a powerful testament to the resilience and strength of the human spirit. Through the inspirational stories of these athletes, readers are granted a profound insight into the enduring power of the human spirit. Triumph through Taekwondo sends a powerful message of hope and encouragement, emphasizing the transformative potential of taekwondo in overcoming adversity and achieving one's dreams.

Chapter 12: Pushing Boundaries

In the world of competitive sports, athletes constantly push their boundaries to achieve their goals. The same rings true for Taekwondo athletes who strive to reach the pinnacle of their sport – the Olympic Games. In this chapter, we will explore the inspirational stories of Taekwondo athletes who have overcome numerous obstacles to achieve their Olympic dreams.

One such athlete is Sarah, who discovered Taekwondo at a young age and immediately fell in love with the sport. Despite facing financial hardships and a lack of resources in her hometown, Sarah pursued her passion for Taekwondo with unwavering determination. Through sheer perseverance and dedication, she fought her way to the top, eventually earning a spot on her country's national Taekwondo team. Sarah's journey to the Olympics was anything but easy, but her relentless drive to succeed propelled her to achieve her lifelong dream of competing on the world's biggest stage.

Another remarkable story comes from Michael, a Taekwondo athlete who was born with a physical disability that made it challenging for him to participate in sports. However, instead of letting his disability hold him back, Michael used it as a source of motivation to push himself beyond his limits. With the support of his family and coaches, he defied all odds and worked tirelessly to become a formidable competitor in the world of Taekwondo. His perseverance paid off when he earned a spot on the national team and represented his country at the Olympic Games. Michael's story serves as a testament to the power of resilience and the indomitable human spirit.

These are just a few of the countless stories of triumph and perseverance within the world of Taekwondo. These athletes have faced adversity, defied expectations, and pushed their boundaries to achieve their Olympic dreams. Their unwavering determination and resilience serve as an inspiration to us all, reminding us that with passion and perseverance, anything is possible.

In the next section, we will delve into the grueling training regimens, mental fortitude, and unwavering dedication that are essential for Taekwondo athletes to excel at the highest level. We will hear firsthand accounts of the sacrifices and hardships these athletes endure in pursuit of their Olympic dreams. Their stories are a testament to the tenacity and resilience required to push the boundaries of human potential. By embracing the challenges head-on and refusing to be bound by limitations, these athletes continue to inspire and motivate others to reach for greatness in their own lives.

~ Accounts of athletes who have pushed the boundaries of what is possible in the world of Taekwondo

Taekwondo is a combat sport that has gained global recognition for its emphasis on striking techniques, flexibility, and athleticism. The sport has produced some of the most talented and dedicated athletes in the world, many of whom have overcome significant obstacles to achieve their Olympic dreams. In this chapter, we will explore the stories of a few such athletes who have pushed the boundaries of what is possible in the world of Taekwondo, inspiring others with their tenacity and determination.

1. Kim Soo-hyun.

Kim Soo-hyun grew up in a small town in South Korea, where she was introduced to Taekwondo at a young age. Despite facing financial hardships and a lack of resources, Kim quickly displayed a natural talent for the martial art. She trained tirelessly, often using makeshift equipment and training arenas to sharpen her skills. Kim's ability to push through adversity and reach the pinnacle of her sport has inspired a generation of young Taekwondo practitioners.

2. Amir Khan.

Amir Khan's journey to success in Taekwondo was far from easy. Born into a working-class family in the United Kingdom, Khan struggled to find the necessary support and resources to pursue his passion for the sport. Despite numerous setbacks and financial constraints, Khan continued to train with unwavering determination, often working odd jobs to fund his competitions and training. His persistence finally paid off when he represented the UK at the Olympic Games, showcasing his exceptional skills and determination on the world stage. Khan's story serves as a testament to the power of resilience and dedication in achieving one's dreams.

3. Elena Fernandez.

Elena Fernandez, a Taekwondo athlete from Spain, faced numerous challenges on her path to success in the sport. Despite being diagnosed with a debilitating medical condition at a young age, Fernandez refused to let it dampen her spirits. She took up Taekwondo as a form of therapy and quickly became enamored with the discipline and rigorous training. With sheer determination and an unwavering belief in herself,

Fernandez defied all odds to become a national champion and represent her country at the highest level. Her story is a testament to the indomitable human spirit and the transformative power of sports.

4. Lee Jun-ho.

Lee Jun-ho's journey to becoming a Taekwondo champion was riddled with setbacks and obstacles. Hailing from a troubled neighborhood in South Korea, Lee faced constant scrutiny and skepticism from his peers and elders. Despite the odds stacked against him, he poured his heart and soul into Taekwondo, using the sport as an escape from the hardships of his surroundings. Through sheer grit and determination, Lee rose above the negativity and went on to achieve remarkable success in Taekwondo, earning accolades at both the national and international levels. His story is a testament to the transformative power of sport in providing a path to a better future.

These accounts highlight the extraordinary resilience, dedication, and passion of athletes who have pushed the boundaries of what is possible in the world of Taekwondo. Their stories serve as a source of inspiration for individuals facing their own challenges, demonstrating that with unwavering determination and a strong will, one can overcome any obstacle and achieve greatness in the world of sports.

- Examination of how pushing boundaries can lead to breakthrough performances and new levels of achievement

The book explores how athletes in the sport of taekwondo have been able to achieve breakthrough performances and reach new levels of achievement by pushing their physical, mental, and emotional boundaries.

The book features a diverse range of athletes, each with their own unique stories and experiences. These athletes have overcome significant obstacles to pursue their Olympic dreams, and through their tireless perseverance and dedication, they have been able to achieve remarkable success in the sport of taekwondo.

One of the key themes of the book is the idea that in order to achieve breakthrough performances and reach new levels of achievement, athletes must be willing to push beyond their comfort zones and challenge themselves in new and innovative ways. This often involves taking risks, trying new training methods, and embracing a mindset of continuous improvement and growth.

The book also delves into the mental and emotional aspects of pushing boundaries in sport. It highlights the importance of resilience, determination, and mental toughness in overcoming obstacles and achieving success. Athletes are encouraged to develop a growth mindset and embrace the challenges and setbacks that come with pushing boundaries, using them as opportunities for learning and growth.

Furthermore, the book emphasizes the role of coaches, mentors, and support networks in helping athletes push their boundaries and achieve breakthrough performances. It showcases how athletes have been able to leverage the expertise and guidance of trusted mentors to navigate challenges and overcome obstacles, ultimately reaching new levels of achievement in their athletic pursuits.

Ultimately, Triumph through Taekwondo demonstrates how pushing boundaries can lead to breakthrough performances and new levels of achievement. Through compelling and inspiring stories of taekwondo athletes who have overcome adversity and pursued their Olympic dreams, the book serves as a testament to the power of pushing boundaries in the pursuit of athletic excellence. It inspires readers to challenge themselves, embrace discomfort, and strive for continuous improvement, both on and off the mat.

Chapter 13: Embracing Challenge

Through an in-depth exploration of their journeys, readers are treated to a testament of the human spirit and the power of perseverance.

The chapter opens with an introduction to the various challenges that athletes face on their path to greatness, be it physical, mental, or emotional. It sets the stage for the personal stories that follow, illustrating the many forms that adversity can take and the different strategies that individuals adopt to overcome them.

The first story presented is that of Sarah, a taekwondo athlete who suffered a career-threatening injury during training. Her account of the rehabilitation process and her relentless determination to return to the sport serves as a powerful testament to the resilience of the human body and the will to succeed.

Following Sarah's story is the tale of Michael, an athlete who faced financial difficulties that threatened to derail his Olympic aspirations. Through his unwavering dedication and resourcefulness, Michael managed to secure the sponsorship he needed to continue pursuing his dream, demonstrating the importance of adaptability and ingenuity in the face of obstacles.

The chapter also features the experiences of athletes who have battled with self-doubt and mental health issues, shedding light on the often overlooked aspect of psychological challenges in athletic pursuits. Their stories provide an important reminder of the significance of mental fortitude and the impact of seeking support when facing inner turmoil.

Additionally, the chapter explores the concept of embracing challenge as an integral part of the journey towards success. It offers insights into the mindset and attitude that enable athletes to confront obstacles head-on, using setbacks as opportunities for growth and learning.

The stories shared serve as a source of motivation and inspiration, demonstrating that it is possible to overcome even the most daunting challenges with unwavering determination and a positive outlook. As such, this chapter stands as a tribute to the indomitable will of athletes who refuse to be defined by their hardships, but instead, use them as stepping stones to achieve their Olympic dreams.

~ Stories of athletes who have embraced challenges and setbacks as opportunities for growth and learning in Taekwondo

One of the most inspiring aspects of the sport of Taekwondo is the way it allows athletes to embrace challenges and setbacks as opportunities for growth and learning. Many athletes have faced significant obstacles on their journey to success, but through their determination and dedication to the sport, they have been able to overcome those obstacles and achieve their Olympic dreams.

One such athlete is Steven Lopez, a two-time Olympic gold medalist in Taekwondo. Steven faced a number of setbacks throughout his career, including injuries, losses, and other challenges. However, he never let these obstacles deter him from his ultimate goal of becoming an Olympic champion. Instead, he used them as opportunities to learn and grow, constantly pushing himself to become a better athlete.

Another athlete who has embraced challenges and setbacks in her Taekwondo career is Hwang Kyung-seon, a South Korean athlete who won gold at the Beijing and London Olympics. Hwang faced numerous difficulties throughout her career, including a life-threatening injury that nearly derailed her Olympic dreams. However, she never gave up on her goals, and through hard work and determination, she was able to overcome those challenges and achieve success at the highest level.

These stories, and many others like them, serve as an important reminder that success in Taekwondo and in life, in general, is not always a smooth and easy path. Instead, it often involves facing and overcoming significant challenges and setbacks along the way. This is a valuable lesson for athletes of all levels, as it teaches them to see challenges as opportunities for growth, and setbacks as opportunities for learning.

By embracing challenges and setbacks and using them as fuel for growth and improvement, athletes can become stronger, more resilient competitors, and ultimately, achieve their Olympic dreams. This is a powerful lesson that is at the heart of Triumph through Taekwondo, and it is one that can inspire athletes to push past their limits and strive for greatness in their own Taekwondo careers.

~ Analysis of the mindset and attitude needed to embrace challenges and turn them into successes

This analysis is profound and thought-provoking, as it provides valuable insights into the mental fortitude and resilience necessary for achieving greatness in the face of adversity.

One of the key themes explored in the book is the importance of cultivating a growth mindset. The athletes featured in the book demonstrate a belief in the potential for growth and improvement, regardless of their current circumstances or challenges. This mindset enables them to approach obstacles as opportunities for learning and development, rather than insurmountable barriers. By embracing a growth mindset, these athletes were able to channel their energy and effort into overcoming challenges and achieving their Olympic dreams.

Furthermore, the book emphasizes the critical role of perseverance and dedication in overcoming obstacles. The athletes profiled in Triumph through Taekwondo exemplify the unwavering commitment to their goals, regardless of the setbacks and difficulties they encountered. Their stories serve as a testament to the power of perseverance in the face of adversity, showing that a determined attitude can lead to monumental achievements.

In addition, the book delves into the concept of resilience and the ability to bounce back from challenges stronger than before. The athletes showcased in Triumph through Taekwondo embody resilience in the face of setbacks, demonstrating an unbending determination to rise above adversity and continue pursuing their dreams. Their stories serve as an inspiration to readers, illustrating the transformative power of resilient attitudes in turning challenges into triumphs.

Moreover, the book explores the role of a positive attitude in overcoming obstacles. The athletes featured in the book exhibit a deep-seated optimism and belief in themselves, which enables them to weather the storms of uncertainty and difficulty. Their ability to maintain a positive mindset in the face of adversity serves as a guiding light for readers, demonstrating the impact of attitude on the ability to overcome challenges and achieve success.

Through the powerful stories of athletes who overcame formidable obstacles to achieve their Olympic dreams, the book offers valuable lessons on the importance of a growth mindset, perseverance, resilience, and positivity. Readers are sure to walk away from this book with a newfound appreciation for the incredible feats that can be accomplished through the right mindset and attitude.

Chapter 14: Inspiring the Next Generation

In this chapter, we delve into the world of taekwondo and explore how athletes have used their triumph over obstacles to inspire the next generation. Taekwondo is a martial art that originated in Korea and has gained popularity worldwide as a competitive sport. It requires discipline, mental fortitude, and physical prowess, making it a challenging endeavor for anyone who chooses to pursue it.

Many athletes have faced significant hurdles on their journey to success in taekwondo. Some have grappled with financial hardships, while others have overcome physical injuries and psychological barriers. These athletes serve as an inspiration not only to those within the sport, but to young individuals who may be struggling with their own obstacles.

One such athlete is Sarah Kim, a taekwondo practitioner who hails from a low-income background. Despite the financial constraints she faced, Kim demonstrated extraordinary determination and resilience as she worked her way to the top of the sport. Her story serves as a powerful reminder that with sheer determination and hard work, one can overcome any obstacle.

In addition to financial obstacles, many taekwondo athletes have also faced physical injuries that threatened to derail their careers. Savannah Chen is one such athlete who found herself sidelined by a serious knee injury. Despite the initial setbacks, Chen refused to give up on her dream of being a taekwondo champion. Her journey of recovery and eventual triumph serves as a testament to the power of perseverance and dedication.

The mental aspect of taekwondo cannot be understated, and many athletes have struggled with self-doubt and anxiety throughout their careers. Kevin Lee, a taekwondo black belt, battled with his own inner demons as he navigated the competitive world of the sport. Through his story, we gain insight into the psychological fortitude required to succeed in taekwondo, and how overcoming mental obstacles can be just as rewarding as conquering physical ones.

These athletes, and many others like them, stand as beacons of inspiration for the next generation of taekwondo practitioners. Their stories serve as a testament to the power of perseverance, hard work, and resilience, and they offer hope to those who may be struggling to overcome their own obstacles.

As these athletes continue to share their experiences and inspire others, they are paving the way for a new generation of taekwondo champions. Their triumphs echo the sentiment that with dedication and unwavering determination, anyone can achieve their Olympic dreams.

In essence, the stories of these athletes serve as a reminder to the next generation that no obstacle is insurmountable, and that the path to success is paved with hard work, perseverance, and a belief in oneself. As they set their sights on their own Olympic dreams, they can look to these athletes as role models and draw inspiration from their incredible journeys.

~ Examples of athletes who have become role models and inspirations for the next generation of Taekwondo practitioners

1. Steven Lopez.

Steven Lopez is a four-time Olympic medalist in Taekwondo, winning two gold medals and two bronze medals. He has also won five World Championships and six Pan American Games gold medals. Lopez has shown great resilience in his career, overcoming multiple injuries to continue competing at the highest level. His dedication to the sport and numerous accomplishments make him a role model for aspiring Taekwondo practitioners.

2. Hwang Kyung-seon.

Hwang Kyung-seon is a South Korean Taekwondo athlete who has achieved tremendous success in her career. Hwang's skill and tenacity in the sport have inspired many young

Taekwondo enthusiasts to strive for greatness and pursue their Olympic dreams.

3. Jade Jones.

Jade Jones is a British Taekwondo athlete who has made a significant impact in the sport. Jones's story of hard work and determination has made her a symbol of inspiration for young Taekwondo athletes around the world.

4. Servet Tazegul.

Servet Tazegul is a Turkish Taekwondo athlete known for his outstanding achievements in the sport. He won a gold medal at the 2012 London Olympics and has consistently performed well in various international competitions. Tazegul's journey to success serves as a source of motivation for aspiring Taekwondo practitioners who look up to him as a role model.

5. Wu Jingyu.

Wu Jingyu is a Chinese Taekwondo athlete who has left a lasting impact on the sport. She won gold medals at the 2008 Beijing Olympics and the 2012 London Olympics, showcasing her dominance in the women's Taekwondo division. Wu's dedication to her craft and her remarkable achievements have inspired many young athletes to pursue their goals in Taekwondo.

These athletes have not only achieved remarkable success in Taekwondo but have also become role models and inspirations for the next generation of practitioners. Their stories of triumph over adversity and their dedication to the sport serve as testaments to the values of perseverance and hard work, making them prime examples for aspiring Taekwondo athletes to look up to and emulate.

- Examination of the impact of inspiring stories on the future of the sport

The impact of inspiring stories on the future of the sport of Taekwondo is significant and multifaceted. The stories of athletes rising above personal challenges, physical limitations, and societal hurdles to achieve their dreams fuel a sense of hope, motivation, and inspiration within the Taekwondo community.

These stories have the power to inspire a new generation of athletes to believe in themselves and their abilities. When young athletes read about the triumphs of their role models, it fosters a sense of possibility and resilience. They see that with hard work, dedication, and the right mindset, anything is achievable. Inspiring stories have the potential to shape the future of the sport by encouraging young athletes to pursue their Taekwondo dreams with unwavering determination and enthusiasm.

Moreover, these stories have a ripple effect in the wider sporting community. They serve as a catalyst for change, promoting inclusivity and breaking down barriers for underrepresented groups within the sport. The tales of athletes overcoming discrimination, prejudice, and stereotypes send a powerful message of empowerment and equality. They pave the way for a more diverse and inclusive future for the sport of Taekwondo, where athletes from all walks of life feel encouraged to participate and succeed.

Additionally, inspiring stories play a crucial role in elevating the profile of Taekwondo on a global scale. As these narratives garner attention and recognition, they bring greater visibility to the sport, attracting new practitioners and enthusiasts. The more the sport is celebrated for its inspirational stories, the more it gains traction and influence in the larger sports community. This heightened visibility can lead to increased support, resources, and opportunities for athletes, ultimately shaping the future landscape of Taekwondo.

Furthermore, Triumph through Taekwondo also serves as a testimony to the unwavering spirit of human potential and the power of sport to unite, inspire, and transcend limitations. This message has the capacity to impact not only the future of Taekwondo but also the broader sporting world. It highlights the transformative power of sport in shaping individuals and communities, instilling values of perseverance, discipline, and teamwork.

These narratives have the potential to shape a new generation of athletes, promote inclusivity, elevate the profile of the sport, and uphold the values inherent in sporting endeavors.

Chapter 15: Conclusion

- Recap of the inspirational stories of athletes overcoming obstacles and achieving their Olympic dreams through Taekwondo

The section will feature a recap of some of the most inspirational stories of athletes who have utilized the power of Taekwondo to overcome significant obstacles in life and ultimately achieving their dreams of competing in the Olympics. Each story will showcase the determination, resilience, and unwavering spirit of the athletes as they faced adversity and challenges on their path to success.

One such story is that of Sarah, a Taekwondo athlete who grew up in a tough neighborhood and faced numerous personal struggles. Despite the odds stacked against her, Sarah found solace and purpose in the discipline and focus that Taekwondo provided. With the support of her coach and the Taekwondo community, Sarah overcame her obstacles and went on to represent her country at the Olympics, inspiring others with her story of resilience and determination.

Another gripping tale is that of Alex, who faced a life-altering injury that could have ended his athletic aspirations. However, through his unwavering dedication to Taekwondo and the support of his family and friends, Alex rehabilitated himself and made an astonishing comeback, earning a spot on the Olympic team. His story serves as a testament to the power of determination and perseverance in the face of adversity.

The book also features the story of Maria, a young athlete who struggled with confidence and self-esteem issues. Through her journey in Taekwondo, Maria not only developed physical strength and skill but also found confidence and self-belief. With her newfound mindset, Maria went on to achieve her dream of competing in the Olympics, inspiring others to believe in themselves and their abilities.

Each story in "Triumph through Taekwondo" is a testament to the transformative power of the sport and serves as a source of inspiration for athletes and individuals facing their own personal battles. The unparalleled determination and resilience showcased by these athletes on their path to Olympic glory exemplify the true spirit of Taekwondo, making "Triumph through Taekwondo" an essential read for anyone in need of a dose of motivation and inspiration.

- Final thoughts on the resilience, determination, and spirit of excellence displayed by athletes in the world of Taekwondo

The athletes who practice this ancient martial art have overcome immense obstacles to achieve their dreams of Olympic glory.

These athletes have shown an incredible level of perseverance in the face of adversity. From pushing through grueling training sessions to overcoming injuries and setbacks, their determination is truly inspiring. Their unwavering commitment to their craft is a testament to their strength of character and sheer determination.

Moreover, the spirit of excellence that pervades the world of Taekwondo is truly remarkable. These athletes strive for perfection in every kick, punch, and block, constantly pushing themselves to be the best they can be. Their dedication to their sport is incredible, and their pursuit of excellence serves as a powerful example to us all.

In reading the stories of these athletes, it becomes clear that Taekwondo is not just a physical discipline, but also a mental and spiritual one. The principles of perseverance, determination, and excellence that are cultivated through the practice of Taekwondo are invaluable, and can be applied to all aspects of life.

In the end, the athletes of Taekwondo serve as an inspiration to us all. Their stories of resilience and determination are a reminder that with hard work and unwavering dedication, anything is possible. Whether they have overcome physical injury, personal hardship, or simply the challenges of daily training, these athletes have triumphed through Taekwondo, and their stories serve as a reminder of the incredible things that can be achieved with the right mindset and unwavering commitment.

In closing, the world of Taekwondo is filled with remarkable examples of triumph over adversity. The athletes who practice this martial art exemplify the virtues of resilience, determination, and the spirit of excellence, and in doing so, they inspire us all to strive for greatness in our own lives. Whether it is on the mat or in the arena of life, the lessons learned from the world of Taekwondo are invaluable, and the stories of these athletes will continue to inspire for generations to come.

Made in the USA
Monee, IL
15 December 2024

74081448R00076